THIS IS A CARLTON BOOK

The Cat Logos and Photographs
© 2005 artlist INTERNATIONAL
Design copyright © 2005
Carlton Books Limited
Text copyright © 2005 Rod Green

This edition published in 2005 by
Carlton Books Ltd
A Division of the Carlton Publishing Group
20 Mortimer Street
London
W1T 3JW

A CIP catalogue for this book is available
from the British Library.

ISBN 1 84442 478 2

Executive Editor: Amie McKee
Art Director: Clare Baggaley
Design: Michelle Pickering
Production: Lisa Moore

Printed and bound in Dubai

THE
CAT

Artlist Collection

THE ORIGINAL
THE CAT
Artlist Collection

CARLTON
BOOKS

Introduction

People have been keeping cats for thousands of years and today they are the world's most popular pets, yet one of their greatest attractions for us is that, even after all this time, we still don't really know them. Stare into their eyes and you can never be quite sure what you might see. Just try it with some of the pictures in this book. Sometimes there is a look of utter bewilderment, sometimes one so endearing it will melt your heart, and sometimes there is a faraway feral look that says, "I'm a wild thing. If you were smaller and I was bigger, I would eat you." If, over the course of time, cats have been domesticated, then maybe someone should have told them so!

In *The Cat*, "strange-ratio" photography – pictures taken using a fish-eye lens (showing 70 per cent body, 30 per cent head) – has been used to capture some of the essence of our favourite pets. More than 50,000 such images have been created as a springboard for the coolest new licensed property from Japan, and this collection shows you the very best.

Nothing creates an air of peace and tranquillity in your home like a contented cat snoozing in front of the fireplace. On the other hand, nothing can create absolute mayhem, shred your curtains and destroy your soft furnishings like a kitten that's just discovered its claws! Cats can be aloof, affectionate, excitable and serene all in less time than it takes to twitch a whisker. All of this and more accounts for our fascination with them, and when you look through this book, we challenge you not to go "Ahhhhhh…"

🐾 Contents

94 Bengal

100 Siberian Forest Cat

102 Russian Blue

116 Mixed Breed

118 Maine Coon

124 Ocicat

130 Mixed Breed

132 Somali

140 Mixed Breed

142 Oriental Shorthair

154 Mixed Breed

156 Munchkin

160 Mixed Breed

162 Scottish Fold

166 Mixed Breed

170 Norwegian Forest Cat

174 Mixed Breed

178 Persian

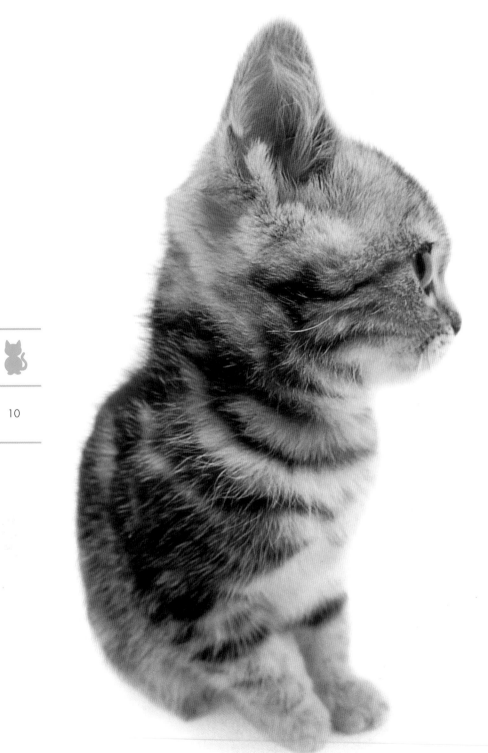

American Shorthair

A large, strong cat, the American Shorthair is at its most magnificent in the dazzling silver-and-black markings of the Silver Tabby, but there are more than 80 other colours and colour combinations within the breed.

At the first large, organized cat show in America, held in Madison Square Garden, New York, in 1895, these cats were simply called Shorthairs, but they later became known as Domestic Shorthairs to distinguish them from foreign breeds.

The very first all-American bred Shorthair was a Black Smoke called Buster Brown, registered in 1904. Buster was an adopted street cat whose "Black Smoke" coat looked a sleek, solid black when he was sitting peacefully, but shimmered when he moved as the lighter colour underneath showed through.

In the early 1960s, American breeders began pressing for a name change, as the "Domestic" label had connotations of a common house cat rather than a pedigree breed and this was seen to be damaging its popularity. The cats finally became the American Shorthair and delighted patriotic breeders when a glamorous Silver Tabby won the 1965 United States Cat of the Year award.

Wheeee! You didn't tell me you had a slide!

So when I was caught sleeping in the pot plant I surrendered like this …

12

… well, how could they resist?

*Keep up the injured paw act –
she's reaching for the cat biscuits.*

Mmmmm … back …

🐾 ... front ...

🐾 ... sideways... I can sleep at any angle.

15

🐾 *It's going to be a brilliant catch!*

🐾 *It's being thrown from all the way across the room!*

Yes! Next time we'll try it with the ball.

*I don't care what you think –
cats can't do karate.*

18

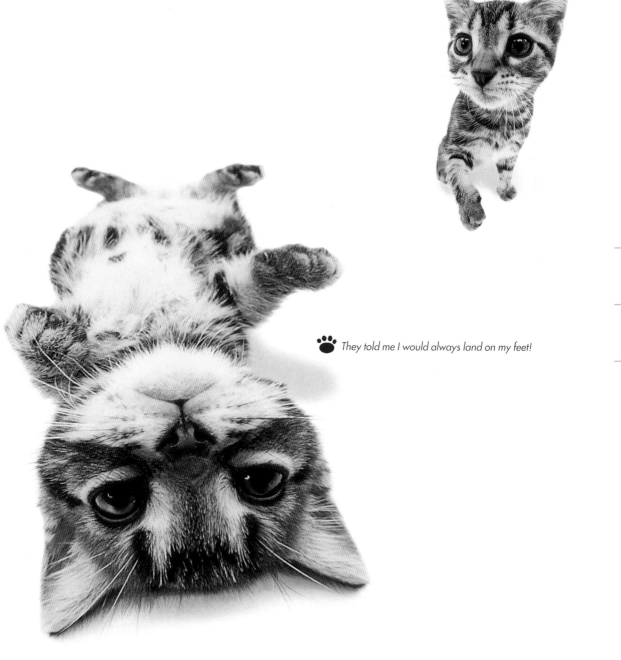

They told me I would always land on my feet!

Look at that aeroplane! If I could fly a plane, no bird would ever be safe again!

Get ready to run – I think they just discovered the remains of our epic battle to the death with the toilet tissue …

22

If he touches my tail, I'm going to get him.

23

 … and he fought the other cat for five whole minutes before he realized he was looking in a mirror!

Abyssinian

Introduced into Britain from Abyssinia, now Ethiopia, in 1868, the Abyssinian almost disappeared at the beginning of the twentieth century, but enthusiasts in France and America helped to keep the breed alive and it is now more popular than ever.

The Abyssinian has a smooth coat that manages to look rough due to the colouration of each of the cat's hairs. Individual hairs have bands of darker colour on a light background giving the overall "ticked" look for which the Abyssinian is famous. This ticking does not appear on the underside of the cat.

Although Abyssinians now come in a wide range of colours, the cats that lived in homes and on the streets in Ethiopian towns were most likely to be a reddish brown in colour, which earned the breed the nickname "hare cat". In France, this colour is still called *lièvre*, which means hare.

Will you please quit sneaking up behind me!

I'm telling you, this is the only way to keep all four paws off the ground.

Be honest: who's got the fluffiest tummy – me or her?

I love him so much. But how do I get him to look at me instead of watching TV?

You'll never reach the cat-biscuit cupboard from there …

Hee-hee! He'll never know what hit him ...

I take my aerobics very seriously.

Did someone just say, "Watch the birdie?"

33

*I'll just take a nap till you're
ready for the next shot.*

🐾 *So I've got a bit of fishy food on my fur … so what?*
They don't have to keep on sniffing like that.

36

Ha-ha! Ha-ha!

 It's really no big deal if you fall off the arm of the couch while you're having a snooze. So why can't he stop laughing?

The first domestic cats

It was in the Middle East that cats first began living close to humans. Cats are known to have lived in villages in Jericho in Israel where a cat's tooth was found dating back to around 9,000 BC. In Cyprus there are no wildcats but cats may have been introduced there, possibly as pets, as cat remains have been found dating back as far as 4,000 BC. It was around this time, too, that cats were living amongst humans in Ancient Egypt, where tombs have been found with pet cats buried alongside their owners.

39

Do you mind? Can't you see I'm washing?

Please, Miss! Can we go out to play now?

Exotic Shorthair

The Exotic Shorthair emerged from a breeding programme in America around 40 years ago, when enthusiasts tried to produce a cat that had a Longhair's coat on the larger, more muscular body of a Shorthair. Instead, what they ended up with was a cat that had a Shorthair's coat on the smaller, more squat body of the Longhair. To differentiate it from what was then known in the United States as the Domestic Shorthair (see page 10), they called the new breed the Exotic Shorthair.

The Exotic's large, round eyes and flat face give it a look of almost permanent surprise that is quite adorable, and this, coupled with its placid nature and easy grooming makes the breed ideal as a house pet. Its coat is not quite as short as that of a true Shorthair and tends to stand out from its body. Exotics seem to enjoy having their fur brushed backwards, from tail to head – something that most cats hate.

*What do you mean I look just
like a Davy Crockett hat?*

Hey! Look at me! If you do this you can't breathe!

Burmese

Although there are records of cats called *rajahs* who lived with Buddhist monks in Burma (now Myanmar) six centuries ago, all modern Burmese cats can trace their ancestry back to a cat called Wong Mau, who was brought from Rangoon to California by US Navy psychiatrist Joseph Thompson in 1930. Wong Mau was crossed with a Siamese to produce the first of what were to become two different types of Burmese. In America, breeders favoured a rounded look to the head and eyes, even a rounded physique, whereas when the Burmese came to Europe, enthusiasts of the breed preferred a more angular look.

At first the Burmese was only ever brown, known as sable, but from the mid 1950s, different colours began to appear. In America, the range of colours felt to be acceptable is not as wide as it is in Europe but, while the differences between the two types continue to grow, American and European Burmese will always have in common an even-tempered, fun-loving nature that is an inherent part of the breed's charm.

 Okay, look, I'll do "the lion" for you ...

... and I'll give you a paw to shake ...

... now can I have one of those fishy treats?

🐾 *What's that buzzy, flying thing?*

🐾 *I don't know, but if it gets any lower,
I'll let you know what it tastes like.*

Have you ever had the feeling that there's something sneaking up behind you?

🐾 *Check out those boxing paws. This kid's going all the way – he's a champ, I tell you!*

Grooming

Grooming your cat is a very important job, especially if your cat has long hair. Cats are very good at keeping themselves clean, but they do appreciate a little help. A cat's coat is waterproof and, when it is cold, it fluffs out, trapping air close to the body, which heats up to help keep the cat warm.

A cat's hair grows at roughly the same rate as human hair but, unlike with humans, it stops once it reaches a certain length. Then, usually in the spring, new hairs begin to grow, pushing the old ones out. When your cats shed their hair, or moult, they like nothing better than for you to help them get rid of the old hair by giving them a gentle brush.

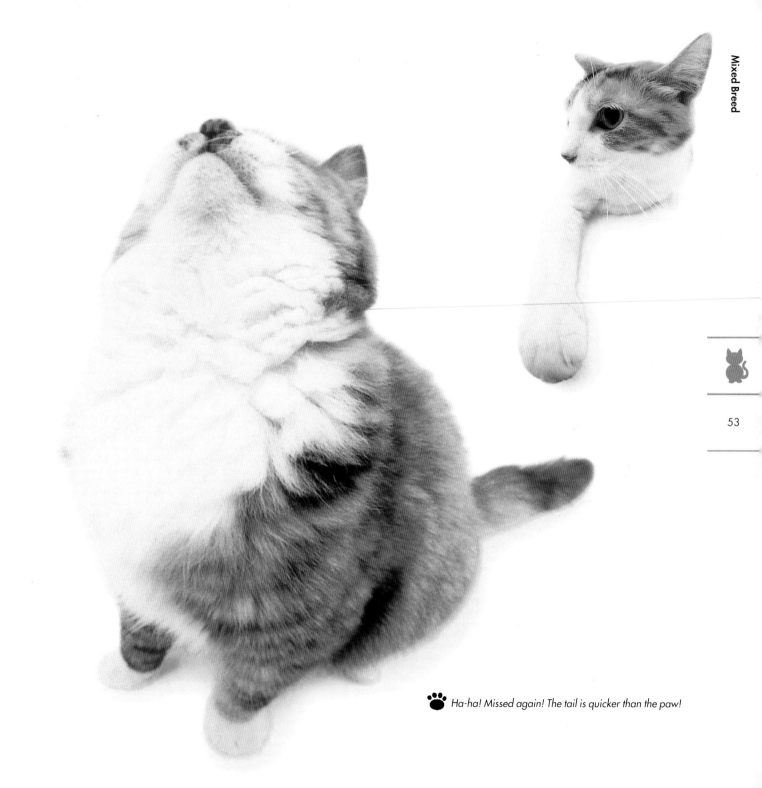

53

Ha-ha! Missed again! The tail is quicker than the paw!

🐾 *... and with one mighty shove, he pushed the Evil One over the cliff ...*

55

🐾 *AAAAAH ... I love this game.*

Pah! No matter how hard I try, that paw just won't stay tucked in when I doze off!

Ragdoll

Ragdolls have earned themselves a strange reputation since they were first bred by Californian Ann Baker in the 1960s. People have come to believe that they feel no pain, have no fear and will not fight with other cats. While these are essentially placid and extremely friendly cats, owners can testify that the myths about the fearless, non-combatant Ragdoll that knows no pain are groundless.

The story of how these sophisticated cats came to be called this rather incongruous name is, however, apparently true. Ann Baker gave the name Ragdoll to the first kittens she bred because, when she picked them up, rather than looking for an affectionate pat or hissing and spitting as other cats might, they simply went limp like rag dolls. Don't be fooled by the name, though – these cats are not limp and listless. Rather, they are large, strong and quite demanding, loving nothing better than to be groomed or petted.

Please tell me I didn't go limp as a kitten ...

Singapura

The Singapura is proof that good things come in small packages. It may not be quite as big as the average cat, but it has a grace and beauty all of its own. Its short coat comes in just one colour, known as Sepia Agouti. The ticked markings on the Singapura's upper body, where the bands of brown colouring on each ivory hair give its coat a distinctive texture, blend smoothly into the pale colour of its underside.

The breed takes its name from the small Southeast Asian island state of Singapore, from where American breeders imported some native cats in 1975. It is thought that their small stature and quiet, almost timid, nature reflect the survival qualities developed by the feral "drain cats" of Singapore. Once you have gained its trust, however, the Singapura is an affectionate and rewarding companion.

*Don't ask where I go at night or what I do.
You <u>really</u> don't want to know ...*

If she claws much harder like that her whole head's going to come off!

64

65

Take it in the bath? Bath? Are you mad?!

Nobody saw me trip over the rug just then, did they?

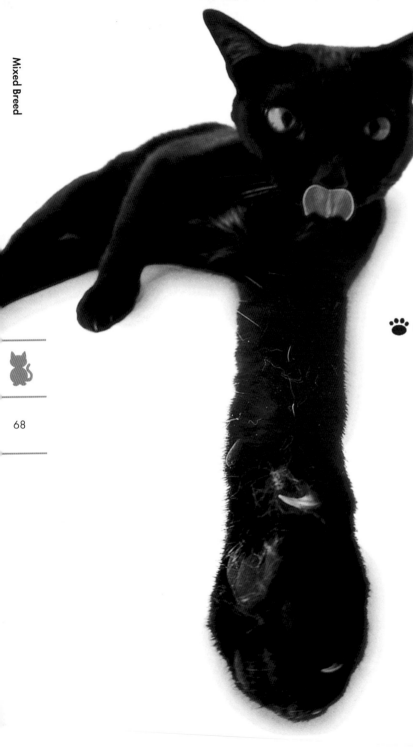

68

Okay, we'll do the pictures, but we want cash up front.

Falsely accused

The usefulness of cats in dealing with rodents meant that they were kept as pets and "working cats" all over the world, but in 1484 the Pope decreed that witches worshipped the devil and kept "familiars" who helped them in their dastardly deeds, the most common familiar being the cat. This led to thousands of people being accused of witchcraft and put to death and, because it was thought that witches could inhabit the bodies of their cats, the cats were tortured and killed too.

Himalayan

Also known as the Colourpoint Longhair, the Himalayan has a colour pattern borrowed from the Siamese, to which it is related. The Siamese was bred with the Longhair in an attempt to produce a cat with a luxuriously long coat but with the "point" markings of a Siamese – darker colour on the face, ears, paws and tail. This colour scheme is also described as "Himalayan", apparently after the markings that appear on mountain rabbits in the Himalayas.

The first Himalayans or Colourpoints appeared in Britain in the 1930s and '40s and were finally accepted as a distinct breed in the mid-1950s, although American breeders had seen some success in trying to achieve the same results. In Europe, a different breed, the Khmer, also existed, but when the international organizations recognized the Colourpoint, the Khmer simply adopted that name, too.

While the breed is now seen in a range of colours, from blue to chocolate and cream, its eyes are always a stunning bright blue.

One of us is called Fluffy, one is Silky and the other is Dusty ...

... we just don't know which is which!

71

72

I just ate half a mouse and hid
the rest under your pillow ...

🐾 He can do impressions, you know ...

 🐾 How's this for a catfish?

She says she's cross because you gave me a kiss and not her …

Any second now she's going to chuck us that mousey toy ...

Mousey toy? Pah! I'm after the necklace!

For the last time, we are all perfectly happy. It just looks like we're frowning!

77

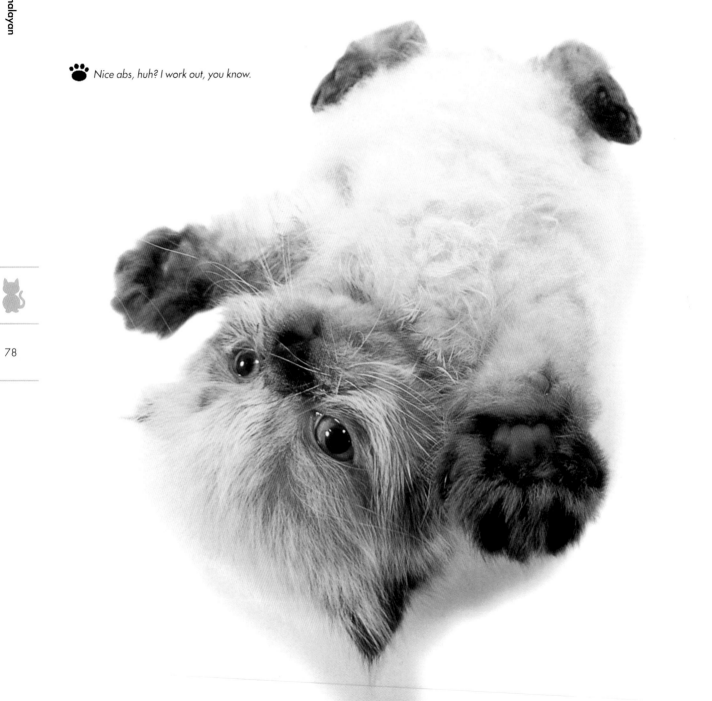

Nice abs, huh? I work out, you know.

Nobody sleeps when I want to play! Time to pounce!

79

American Curl

Having emerged only within the last 25 years
or so, the American Curl is one of the newest
cat breeds. This cat is characterized by its
striking ears, which curl backwards away from
its face, making it look as though it's facing
into a stiff breeze. American Curl kittens are
born with straight ears, but their ears begin to
curl when they are about a week old. Although
the ears may then straighten again, they will
usually curl back once more and stay curled
once the kittens are about four months old.

There are both long-haired and short-haired
versions of the Curl, although the cats that
were originally bred in California were all
long-haired. All American Curls have tails as
long as their bodies and the long-haired's tail
is a thick, feathery plume. Curls appear in
almost every variation of colour, and
combination of colours, imaginable.

Didn't know cats could wink, did you?

The trouble is, once you've washed your
whiskers, they just kind of do their own thing ...

Mummy says we're little devils – I can't think why ...

I thought only dogs did the "play dead" trick!

85

Okay, everybody, on three do the big, sad eyes! One, two, three! They always feed us when we do the big, sad eyes!

Landing on their feet

The old saying that "cats always land on their feet" is not always true, but cats are incredibly agile and do have a special "sense" that helps them to twist around in mid-air if they need to. Cats can not only see that they are falling, but feel, through the highly sensitive cavities of their inner ear, that their balance is being affected. When cats' ears tell their brain that they are in trouble, the brain triggers an automatic reflex that twists their heads around. The rest of their body then follows and, nine times out of ten, cats will land on their feet.

Did anyone see where I left that spongey ball thing?

🐾 *As soon as I've finished washing, I'm off.*

90

🐾 *You can't stop me ...*

... *Byeeeeeeeeeeee!*

🐾 *So does the little bird ever come out of its cage?*

🐾 *Nope – and I've been watching for days ...*

Bengal

Although it sounds as though it should be directly descended from some kind of miniature tiger, the Bengal actually first appeared in America in the 1970s. A scientist at the University of California, who was studying disease resistance in the Asian Leopard Cat, bred these cats with others, eventually producing what became known as the Bengal. The university cats were passed on to Mrs Jean Mill, who had some experience with the Leopard Cat breed, and she registered the first of the Bengals in 1983.

In common with many American breeds, Bengals are large, muscular cats. The Brown Spotted variety most closely resembles its Leopard Cat ancestors. As a new breed, the Bengal is still relatively rare, but its soft, luxurious coat is so pleasing to the touch, and its affectionate nature so appealing, that anyone lucky enough to have one would surely never want any other breed.

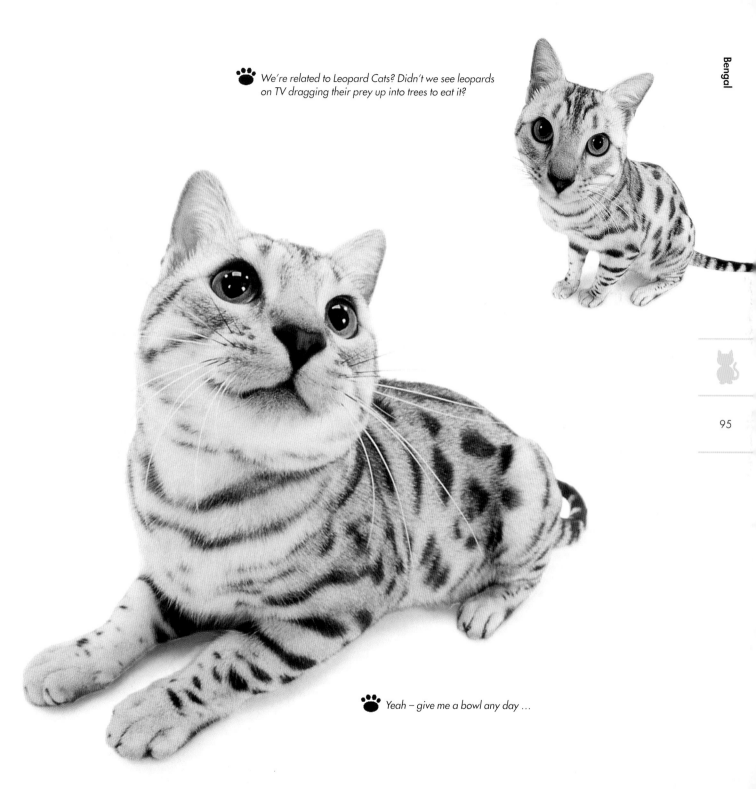

We're related to Leopard Cats? Didn't we see leopards on TV dragging their prey up into trees to eat it?

Yeah – give me a bowl any day …

95

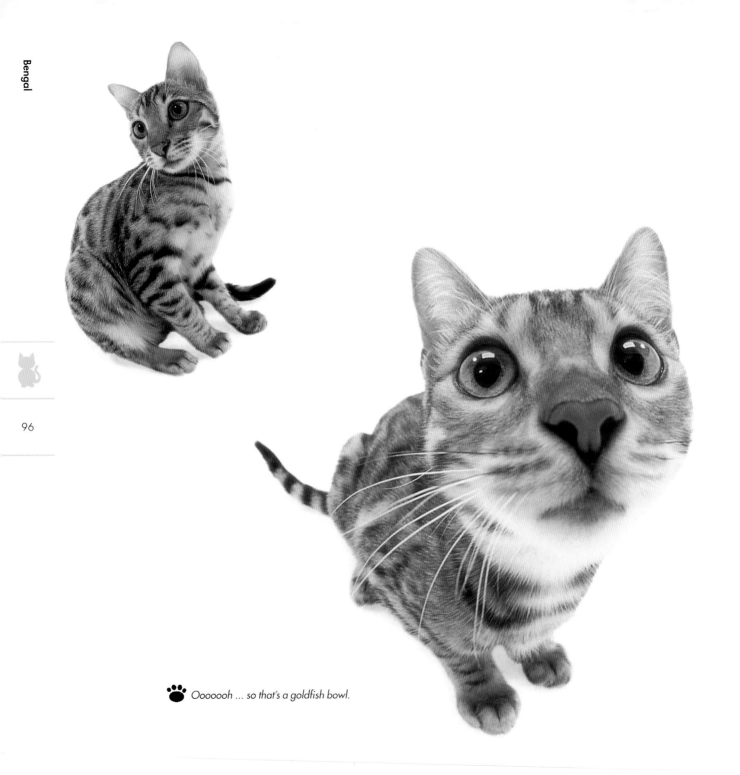

Ooooooh ... so that's a goldfish bowl.

With a bit of a run at it, I reckon I could make it straight up those curtains …

 Would that be such a bad thing?

Siberian Forest Cat

If you lived in Siberia, where the Soviet winter is famously long and cruelly cold, you would want a big, thick coat, possibly two, and that's exactly what the Siberian Forest Cat has got. The long, oily hair of its topcoat is designed to keep out the worst of the rain and snow while its dense undercoat blocks the fiercest of winds.

Of course, to carry two such heavy coats, you have to be big and strong, and the Siberian has a large muscular build, although its powerful physique does not prevent it from being both energetic and surprisingly agile. Because they are so well equipped for the great outdoors, Siberians do not feel entirely at home cooped up in a warm house. They can tolerate heat when it suits them and enjoy human company when they choose to, but they're not generally the sort of cats to keep you company on the sofa in the evening.

While Siberians have existed in Russia for many years, it was not until 1990, when enthusiasts brought them to America, that this imposing breed began to gain true recognition.

I don't care what anyone else thinks –
I'm the most glamorous cat around here.

Russian Blue

The Russian Blue has been known variously throughout the years as the American Blue, Spanish Blue, Maltese Blue and the Archangel Cat, a name that betrays its true ancestry. These gentle, sometimes shy cats were brought to the West in the nineteenth century by sailors from the Russian port of Archangel, close to the Arctic Circle. They were believed to bring great good luck in Russia, where owning one was seen as something of a status symbol. One Blue, called Vashka, was the favourite pet of Tsar Nicholas II.

In all the time that these cats have been bred in the West, only one thing about them has changed. The original Blues had orange eyes, whereas the modern version has vivid emerald-green eyes. All-black and all-white versions have appeared, notably in New Zealand, but for the purists, only the beautifully lustrous, blue coat of the original will do.

102

 Is it milk time yet? I'm parched.

*You can tell by his twitches that he's dreaming
about the giant purple mouse again.*

Come back! This time I really will let you swat the next ant.

No. I wouldn't want to do it anyway.

104

What is that awful noise?

Run! It's the vacuum cleaner!

Hypnotizing him was easy, but how do you do that wakey-wakey, finger-snappy bit?

Then I do this and it's all over for you ... if you're a moth.

110

*They're all just staring at nothing, you know.
They do it to try to freak me out.*

See? Spinning round in circles on the floor is cool!

*Coffee with cream, please,
and hold the coffee ...*

*I'll trade you a play with my duck
for ten minutes in your castle ...*

115

 *He must think I'm crazy – this
castle is worth a million ducks!*

Marking its territory

When you see cats rubbing themselves against a tree or a fence post, it might look like they're enjoying a good scratch, but they're actually leaving a message for all other cats in the area to say "I've been here" or "This is where I live".

Cats have scent glands on their heads, necks and near their tails, which leave a trace that other cats can smell. Your cats might lovingly rub themselves against you when you arrive home, but they are actually "marking" you, too. That's to tell other cats that you belong to them – and you thought that your cats belonged to you!

Shiny floor or not, no one ever expects me to come shooting past like this.

Ahhh … now for a snooze …

Maine Coon

The playful and affectionate Maine Coon has become one of the world's most popular breeds, despite losing ground to the Persians in the early part of the twentieth century.

The breed's unusual name comes from Maine, America's "Pine Tree State" on the eastern seaboard, where this cat is thought to have originated, and from the fact that people at one time believed that feral cats in Maine had mated with native racoons. That, of course, was a complete myth, but the name stuck nevertheless. Maine Coons probably evolved as a result of local cats breeding with foreign types that arrived in the area aboard trading ships in the nineteenth century.

Certainly, the Maine Coon retains one of the major characteristics of American cats in that it is a large breed, many examples growing to more than twice the weight of an average household cat.

🐾 *Want to fight?*

🐾 *What are you looking at?*

🐾 *Come on! Give it your best shot!*

No, I won't play with you until you apologize for biting my tail.

He reckons this is the easiest way to tunnel up under a duvet while you're asleep …

122

123

Ocicat

First reared in America as a cross between Siamese and Abyssinian breeds (see page 24), the Ocicat takes its name from the ocelot, a small South American leopard that has been prized for its luxurious coat since the time of the Aztecs. Hunting and the loss of its natural habitat to deforestation have sadly made the ocelot an endangered species.

The markings of the first Ocicat kittens (bred in Michigan in the 1960s) were what inspired its breeders to adopt the name: the cat's spots and stripes closely resemble the markings of the ocelot. Happily, the Ocicat, although still quite rare, is not facing the same danger of extinction as its namesake.

These are extremely easy cats to befriend. They have a playful nature and a love of curling up in a warm lap – although the male, which is much larger than the female, can be quite a heavy couch partner. Ocicats are also famous for being far more tolerant towards children than are many other breeds, making them ideal family pets.

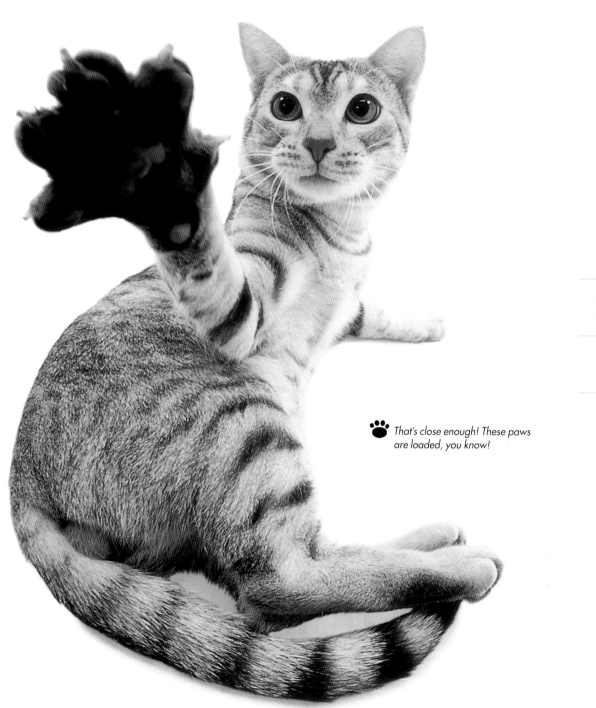

125

That's close enough! These paws are loaded, you know!

They call us the disco cats …

🐾 … *And I play harmonica …*

🐾 … *And I'm on keyboards.*

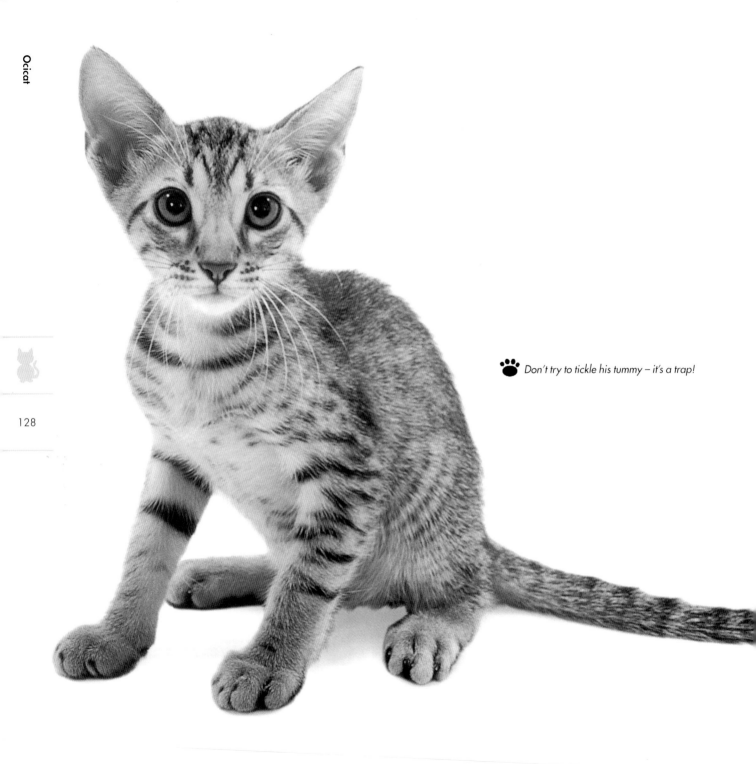

Don't try to tickle his tummy – it's a trap!

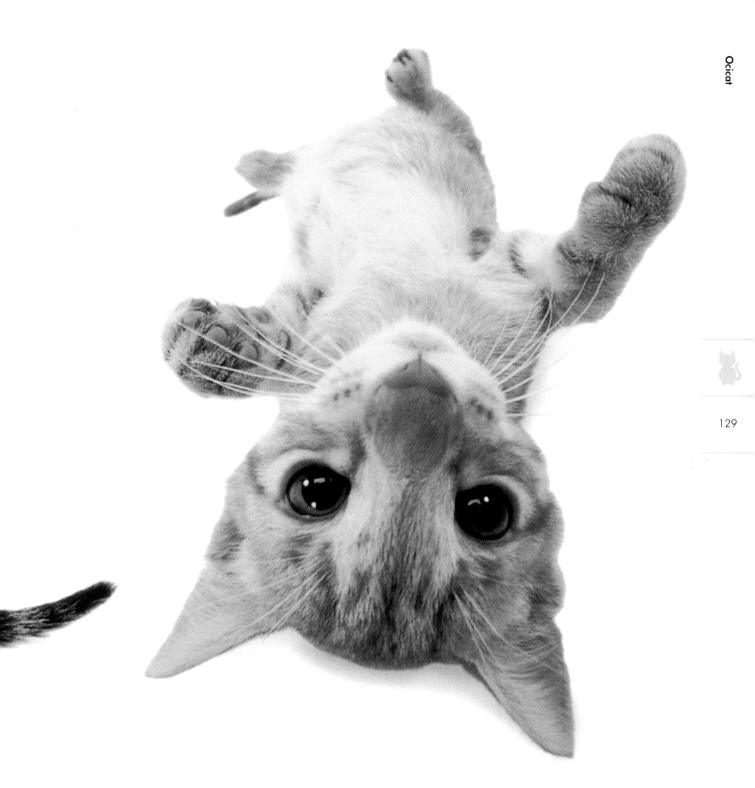

130

Ancient Egyptian favourites

The cat was undoubtedly the last of the wild animals to be domesticated, although some people would maintain that even today cats remain thoroughly independent. The Ancient Egyptians used cats to guard their grain stores from rodents and to help keep their homes free from other such vermin, but they also trained cats to help them hunt birds.

Such was their affection for cats that they even worshipped a cat goddess called Bastet. They also mummified cats, giving them a proper burial when they died. The cats' owners would shave off their own eyebrows to show their grief. In one Egyptian cat cemetery more than 300,000 cat mummies were discovered!

131

Ha! You can't keep that camera strap out of my reach forever, you know!

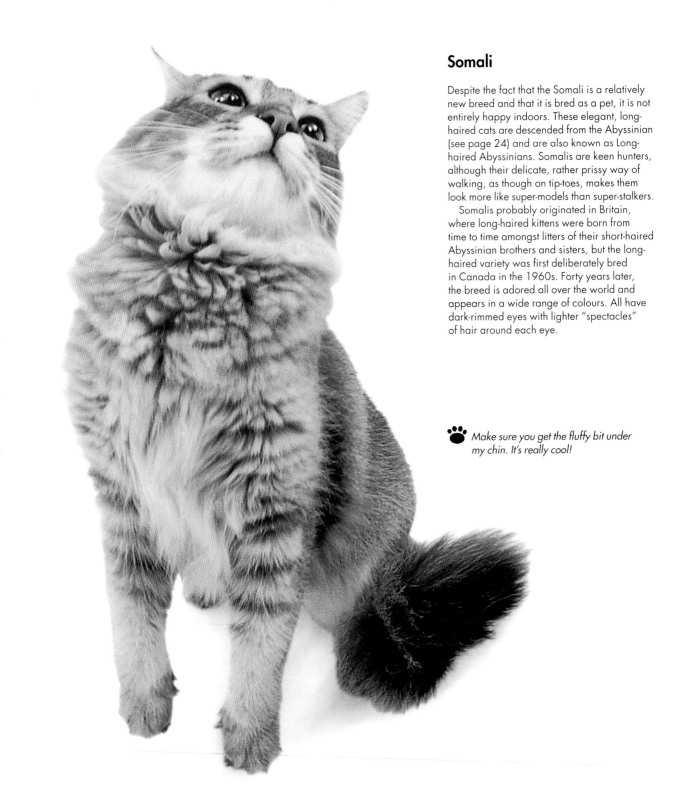

Somali

Despite the fact that the Somali is a relatively new breed and that it is bred as a pet, it is not entirely happy indoors. These elegant, long-haired cats are descended from the Abyssinian (see page 24) and are also known as Long-haired Abyssinians. Somalis are keen hunters, although their delicate, rather prissy way of walking, as though on tip-toes, makes them look more like super-models than super-stalkers.

Somalis probably originated in Britain, where long-haired kittens were born from time to time amongst litters of their short-haired Abyssinian brothers and sisters, but the long-haired variety was first deliberately bred in Canada in the 1960s. Forty years later, the breed is adored all over the world and appears in a wide range of colours. All have dark-rimmed eyes with lighter "spectacles" of hair around each eye.

Make sure you get the fluffy bit under my chin. It's really cool!

Want to see how I fluff my tail?

133

Cool! … Aw, nuts! Did I just miss the photo?

I know it looks silly, but I love it when my tail tickles my back.

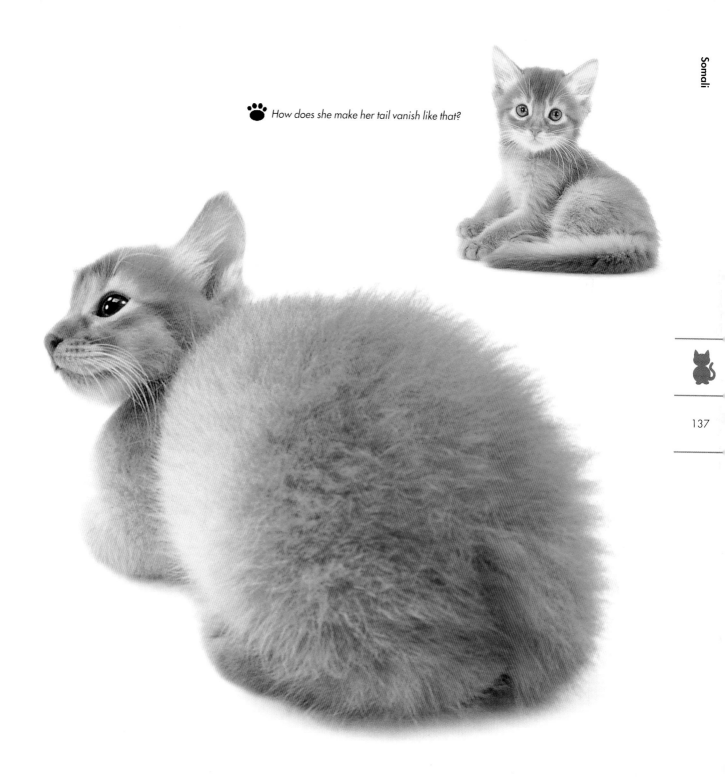

How does she make her tail vanish like that?

I smell foooooood ...

He thinks he's a yeti ...

The cat's sixth sense

Cats are often said to have a "sixth sense" that warns them of impending danger, and there is plenty of evidence to show that they are sensitive to the onset of natural disasters. On 7 May, 1976, cats in the Friuli region of northern Italy began scrabbling to get out of houses during the day. At 9.00pm a massive earthquake hit the area, devastating 11 villages. In March 1944, a cat called Toto woke his owner during the night by scratching at his face. The man and his wife left their home just before Mount Vesuvius erupted and their house was destroyed by lava.

🐾 *Check out those stripes!*
So is he a tiger or not?

141

Oriental Shorthair

Playful and demanding of attention, the Oriental Shorthair looks and behaves very much like a Siamese, with which it shares its ancestry. It has the same short coat and the same narrow, triangular face with pointed ears that extend the line of the face outwards. And like the Siamese, it has an inquisitive nature and a way of calling for attention in a very loud voice. It also retains the Siamese characteristics of small, round paws and hind legs that are noticably longer than its front ones. However, the Oriental does not normally have the Seal Point markings usually associated with Siamese, nor, with one remarkable exception – the Oriental White – does it have the latter's blue eyes.

In the 1950s, attempts to breed different varieties of Oriental in the USA and Britain (where these cats were once known as the far less glamorous Foreign Shorthair) led to the establishment of what are now distinctly different breeds, such as the Havana Brown.

Hey! I can see myself in your camera thingy!

144

 ... and the rat I caught was this high!

He tells a great story – but you can't believe a word of it!

He bit my paw!

146

No I didn't! He stuck it in my
mouth while I was yawning!

148

If she keeps on eating her own tail, will she eventually disappear completely?

149

Then you pull your back leg up like this and you can play air guitar with it!

I hope you're not expecting me to do all that silly stretching and stalking, too?

154

The cat festival of Ypres

Every three years in Ypres in Belgium, there is
a cat festival, where the people of Ypres
parade through the streets dressed as cats. In
a ceremony that dates back to the twelfth
century, when the procession was used to rid
the area of witches, a giant statue of Bastet,
also known as the Norse goddess Freya, is
towed through the town to the Cloth Tower.
Here, there is a ceremonial burning of witch
effigies before the parade's cat queen climbs
to the top of the Cloth Tower with her jesters.
Until 1817, when the practice was outlawed,
real cats were hurled to their deaths from the
tower. Nowadays, thankfully, they throw velvet
cats down to the crowds below instead.

155

Wow! I never knew you could see so far inside an ear!

Munchkin

Munchkins have been a recognized cat breed for more than 10 years but they still fuel the fires of one of the cat world's greatest debates. Should the deliberate breeding of this type have been allowed?

Munchkins first appeared in Louisiana more than twenty years ago. At that time, they were abnormal cats with unusually short legs. Miniature breeds of dog have been produced for centuries, and there are inherent physical problems with many of them, but the Munchkin was the first dwarf cat. It is to be hoped that the more supple body of the cat will be better able to cope should its shorter legs tend to cause the sort of hip and spinal problems sometimes seen in small dogs.

The Munchkin's short legs may be a freak of nature, but owners maintain that the cats are healthy and happy, clowning like kittens even when they should be old enough to know better. Munchkins come in many different colours and have bushy coats that require a good deal of grooming, but their endearing personalities help to make this less of a chore and more of a silly game!

I may look sweet and fluffy, but I'm a tiger inside!

157

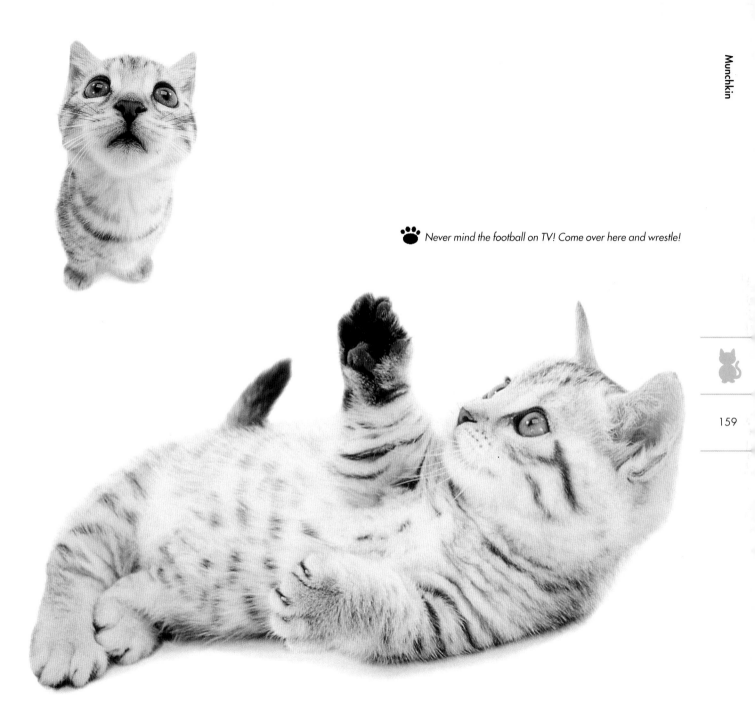

Never mind the football on TV! Come over here and wrestle!

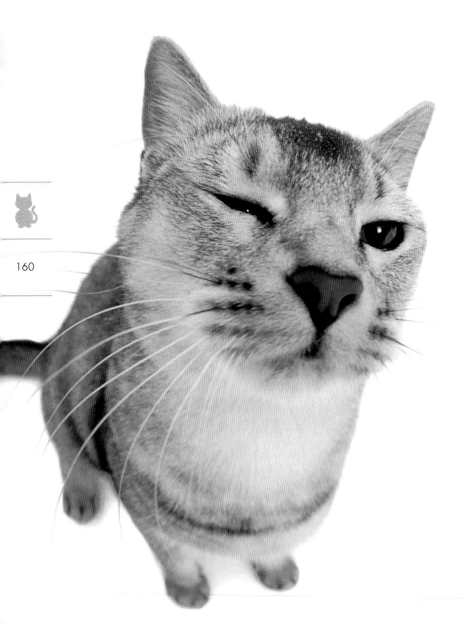

Wildcats and domestic cats

The cat family can be divided into two main groups: Panthera, which includes the lion, tiger and leopard – the big cats that can roar – and Felix, which includes the puma, ocelot, lynx and the wildcats from which our domestic cat, *Felis catus* is descended.

Wildcats – not to be confused with feral cats, which are domestic cats living wild – inhabit a wide range of environments from the forests of Scotland through Europe to the jungles and deserts of Africa, the Middle East and Asia. They are generally much larger than domestic cats, but are so closely related that they can and do interbreed when wildcats find themselves living close to towns or villages.

Getting up the tree was easy ...

... but getting down again was ... exhausting!

Scottish Fold

Although it is thought that the Scottish Fold may be descended from Chinese cats that were brought to Britain in the late nineteenth century, the modern Scottish Fold can safely trace its ancestry back only as far as the 1960s in Tayside in Scotland.

The cats that were brought to Britain by traders more than a century ago caused something of a sensation when they arrived, as no cat breed had previously been seen with ears that folded forwards over its head. The novelty appears to have worn off, however, as this feature seemed to die out until a Perthshire farm cat called Susie produced a kitten with flattened ears and the Scottish fold breed was established.

Apart from looking like cats that have been wearing hats, the other notable features of Folds are their large, round eyes, stocky back legs and thick tail. Their fur is short and they appear in all different colours and patterns.

We didn't mean to shred your slippers ...

 ... they attacked us!

Hanging by one paw from the window ledge ...
I could use some help here, guys ... Guys?!

Hunting or playing?

All cats have a natural instinct to hunt prey. That doesn't mean that all cats will go out and bring home mice, frogs or small birds, but many will. Often they will present these trophies to you because they want you to see how clever they have been, but it's difficult to feel proud of your pets when they drop a half-dead mouse at your feet!

Cats that spend most of their time indoors need furry or feathered toys to help them satisfy their hunting instinct. They will pounce, capture and "kill" even a ping-pong ball just as though it were real prey, so it's vital that you keep a few toys around to help your cat lead a happy life.

Mmmmmm ... if only all ducks were so easy to catch.

167

Is it my turn for a photo?

I'm not sure I'm ready yet.

Have you ever had one of those mornings when you just couldn't get your eyes open?

Norwegian Forest Cat

Marauding Viking raiders, storming ashore from their longboats, swinging their great battleaxes and laying whole villages to waste, hardly seem suitable candidates for the title of the world's foremost cat-fanciers. Not all Viking travellers were ferocious warriors, however. The Vikings established trade routes to Europe and Asia, bringing home, amongst other things, cats. That was around 1,000 years ago, but the breeds that flourished in the Vikings' Scandinavian homelands – large cats with long, thick fur to see them through the harsh winters – were undoubtedly the ancestors of today's Norwegian Forest Cat.

The "Wegie", as it also sometimes known, is a strong, clever cat, happy to live indoors but happier still outside, where its dense double coat – a water-resistant top layer and a warm, woolly, bottom layer – keeps out the worst weather, and where it can indulge its passions for climbing and hunting. Wegies have even been known to go fishing in brooks.

171

If you were a mouse, I'd have you on toast!

She wouldn't be sleeping so happily if she knew we'd got her surrounded!

Prehistoric Ancestors

The kitten that you see chasing butterflies in the garden or losing a mighty battle with a ball of twine may not look like one of the most highly evolved carnivores on the planet, but we can trace his ancestry back many millions of years. The cat family developed from a species called *Pseudoailanus* (meaning "false cat"), which lived around 25 million years ago. This creature had fur and teeth, ate only meat and walked on tip-toe just as that kitten in the garden does.

174

 It's no good. I can't do it …

 … Nor can I. How on earth did the hedgehog manage it?

Come and play or I'll claw my way up your trouser leg.

176

Who'd have thought that switching
on the TV was so easy?

Persian

Europeans knew nothing of the noble Persian until the early seventeenth century when the breed, also know simply as the Longhair, was first imported from Persia (now Iran) to Italy. Its long, luxurious coat quickly made it a very fashionable house pet among the chic social elite in its new homeland.

With its large head, drooping cheeks and big round eyes, the Persian often appears to have a grumpy expression. In fact, these cats are normally quite placid and affectionate – a result of having been bred as house pets for so long. While some cat lovers might think the grumpy look – accentuated in the tabby by "frown-line" markings on the forehead – rather unfortunate, others positively covet it. The flat-faced characteristics are especially prized in what are known as "Peke-faced Persians", which are bred specifically to look like Pekingese dogs.

*Sorry. He says the draught
keeps blowing him over ...*

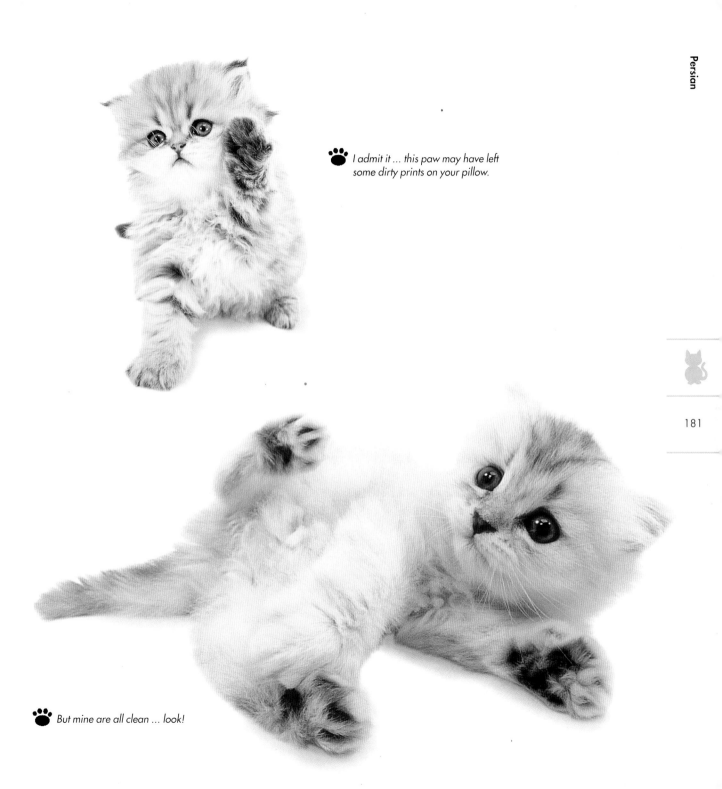

I admit it ... this paw may have left some dirty prints on your pillow.

But mine are all clean ... look!

He's still not figured out that for running it's "paws on the ground."

184

Hey! The bird went up in the air! They can fly!

185

 That's just not fair!

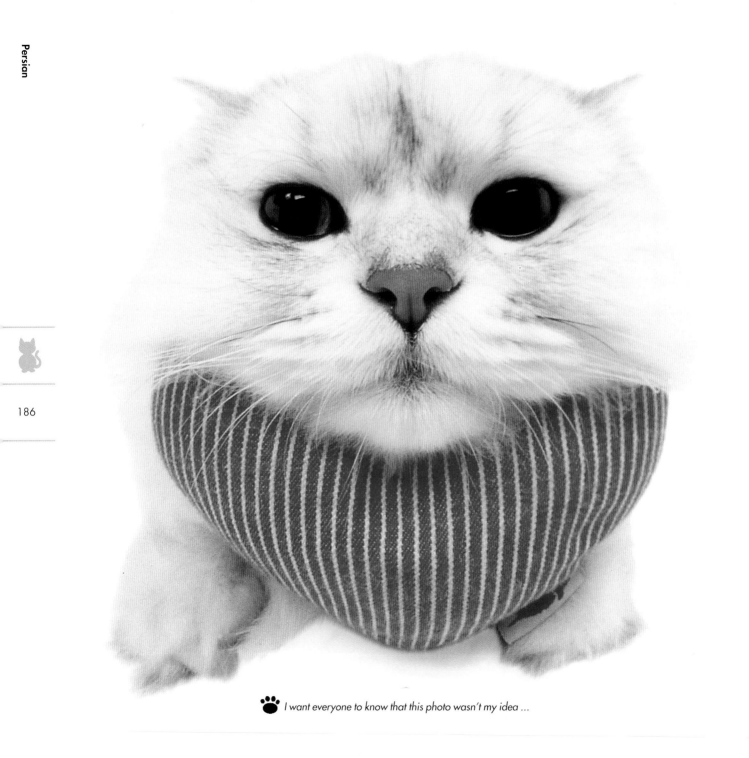

I want everyone to know that this photo wasn't my idea ...

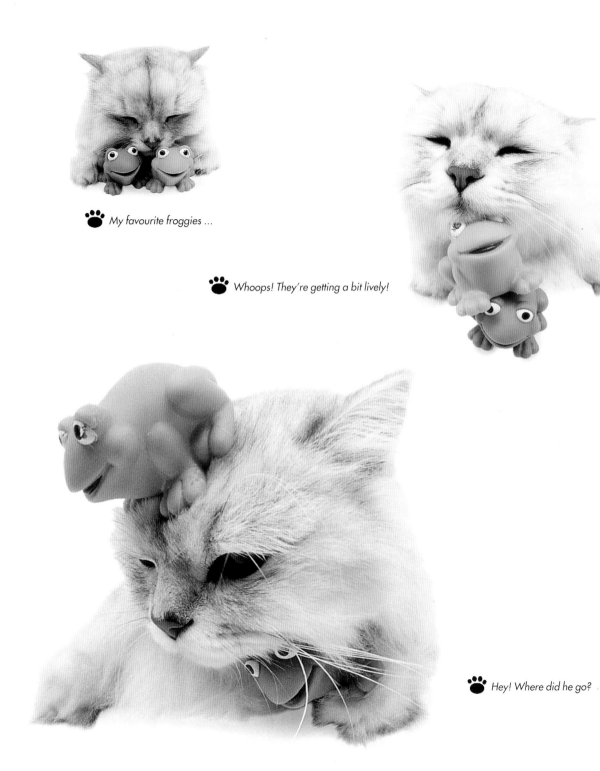

🐾 *My favourite froggies ...*

🐾 *Whoops! They're getting a bit lively!*

187

🐾 *Hey! Where did he go?*

189

... then roll over, show them all your claws and maybe a few teeth
and no one will ever try to move you from in front of the fire.

I don't know why you couldn't sit still for a proper photo …

190

 There was an ant, I tell you! I think I got him!

Is this the way out?

Did you hear the one about the three-legged dog who couldn't pass a lamp post without falling over? Ha-ha-ha!